THE
YORKSHIRE
DALES

Biographies and Acknowledgements

Photographs by E. A. Bowness, Norman Duerden & David Tarn

Ted Bowness was born into an old Cumbrian family and now lives in a South Lakeland village. He sold his first photograph to *Motorcycle Magazine* and later established his own picture library, specialising in Cumbria and the Yorkshire Dales. In 1978 he produced a book of his photographs which sold over 100,000 copies.

To Maureen of the Eagle Eye
Naturalist, artist and writer **Norman Duerden** took his first nature pictures with an ancient hand-and-stand plate camera. Two decades later he began a long series of wildlife colour studies; these have been used by the BBC and as illustrations for his many books on Scotland, the Dales and natural history. A former College Vice Principal and Fellow of the Royal Society of Arts, he now lives in retirement in the Ribble Valley.

For Christine, my long-suffering wife, and for Dominic and Sara
David Tarn lives with his young family in North-East England, within easy access of the Yorkshire Dales and other areas of scenic beauty. He is a self-taught photographer who turned his hobby into a career in 1993. He now runs his own picture library and undertakes photographic commissions.

Text by Anna Newland

For Vic
Anna Newland has lived near London all her life, but takes every opportunity to escape to the Yorkshire Dales to indulge her hobbies of walking, painting and photography.

With grateful thanks to Fiona Rosher, Debbie Allen, Denny Minnit, Sue Wood and Dave Jones.

Picture Credits
E.A. Bowness pp. 25, 31, 35, 36, 45, 51, 56, 59, 62, 65, 68, 73, 77, 94, 100, 104, 109, 112, 115, 116, 117, 120, 124, 125, 129, 132, 133, 134, 135, 136, 137, 138 (© **English Life Publications Ltd**), 139, 141, 144, 145, 146, 147, 148, 149, 152, 154, 156, 157, 158, 160, 161, 163, 164, 167, 172, 178, 180, 181, 183, 186, 195. **Norman Duerden** pp. 18, 20, 21, 22, 23, 26, 27, 37, 40, 57, 78, 86, 91, 92, 95, 96, 97, 106, 108, 114, 128, 130, 131, 140, 171, 173, 185, 187, 189, 193. **Tim Grevatt** p. 165. **Anna Newland** pp. 39, 50, 52, 53, 81, 121, 179. **Peter W. Robinson** pp. 113, 127, 159. **David Tarn** pp. 14, 15, 17, 19, 24, 30, 33, 34, 38, 41, 43, 44, 46, 47, 49, 58, 61, 63, 64, 67, 69, 72, 75, 76, 79, 80, 83, 87, 89, 90, 93, 99, 101, 105, 107, 119, 142, 153, 162, 170, 175, 176, 177, 182, 188, 190, 191, 192. **The Bridgeman Art Library** p. 197.

ISBN 0 75252 930 7

First published in 1999 by
SIENA
Queen Street House
4 - 5 Queen Street
Bath BA1 1HE

Copyright 1999 © Siena

This is a Siena Book

Produced for Siena by Foundry Design and Production, Crabtree Hall, Crabtree Lane, Fulham, London SW6 6TY.

THE YORKSHIRE DALES

PHOTOGRAPHS BY
E. A. BOWNESS, NORMAN DUERDEN, DAVID TARN

NORMAN DUERDEN

Text by Anna Newland

SIENA

Contents

Contents by Region

INTRODUCTION

The curlew calls and the wind sighs, high up where the wild and lonely moors meet the sky. Here, five of the main rivers of the Yorkshire Dales have their beginnings, sweeping down from the high watershed of the Central Pennines to flow through some of the most wonderful countryside in England.

The rivers Ribble, Swale, Wharfe and Aire lend their names to the best known dales, each of them with its own distinct character; the river Ure runs through Wensleydale. They all cut through the thick white mass of rock, known as the Great Scar Limestone, which makes up the bones and some of the most outstanding features of the Dales landscape. Formed millions of years ago by a tremendous agglomeration of the bodies of the small creatures who swam and died in their warm tropical sea, it still displays their fossilised shapes.

Softer shales and sandstones, more subject to erosion, were later deposited, building up layers interspersed with the limestone over a long expanse of time. These layers were eventually topped by a thick, dark layer of 'Millstone Grit' – so called because of its widespread use for millstones.

A dramatic climatic change brought the ice sheets and the grinding glaciers which inched their way inexorably through the valleys, smoothing away any jutting spurs and carving the wide 'U'-shaped dales which we see today. With the ending of the last Ice Age, the glaciers retreated, leaving smooth hillsides and flat valley floors, and depositing the erratics, moraines and drumlins which are a feature of any glaciated landscape. Water pouring through the dales wrought its own changes, dissolving the softer rocks at a faster rate than the hard limestone, creating shelves and terraces, caves and pot-holes.

This is the remarkable landscape that nature has fashioned, although man too has shaped and marked this land. Life must have been harsh here, and Neolithic people were reluctant to venture far into the desolate uplands. They sheltered in southern caves, leaving the remains of bears and of the reindeer who would have grazed the mosses and grasses which had appeared on the sub-arctic, tundra-like landscape, so much different

from that of today. Later, grassland and trees colonised the area to create the more familiar scene which now exists.

The remains of some of the early people to settle here date from the Bronze Age. A trading people who laid crude field boundaries and marked out the first of the many paths and tracks which traverse this land. Then the advent of the Celts from the west ushered in the Iron Age, and plentiful evidence of their culture and settlements can still be identified in many parts.

The Romans also came to Yorkshire, bequeathing their long straight roads, and Anglian settlers introduced place names still used today in the southern Dales, where they found a rich soil, well-suited to their arable farming needs. The Danes came marauding – and then settled, leaving a legacy of Norse names in the villages of the higher ground further north.

The last wave of incomers came after 1066. The Norman tyranny was fiercely opposed but eventually enforced, and the invaders set about taking over land and forest for hunting, and building great castles such as Richmond and Bolton. Under the Normans, the power of the monasteries and abbeys grew, and theirs was undoubtedly the greatest influence in the Dales.

Monks of the Cistercian order first settled here in the 12th century. Quick to recognise the value of the wool trade they ruthlessly took over vast tracts of land on which to graze their enormous numbers of sheep. With this repression and dispossession of the poor, the monks came to be feared and hated; indeed there are some who assert

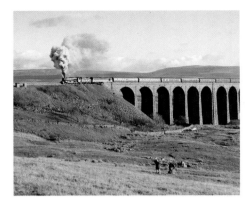

that Robin Hood championed the poor here, from a base in Barnsdale forest, rather than from Sherwood.

The grip of the Monasteries lasted for 400 years, ending abruptly and devastatingly with Henry VIII's Dissolution. Social change came to the Dales with new landowners and merchants who prospered from the wool and cloth produced here, and from the extensive lead mines. They built the mills, a number of fine houses, and many cottages to house the rising population of miners and mill workers.

At the end of the 18th century, a new kind of invader came: the first tourists were inspired by the awakening national interest in the natural world. The middle classes arrived with the leisure to come and marvel at the richness and beauty of the lovely Dales, with their romantic ruins, mellow stone cottages and breathtaking scenery.

Artists and poets also came: Edwin Landseer sought inspiration for his romantic pictures, as did Thomas Girtin. Turner also painted here, delighting in the wonderful light so

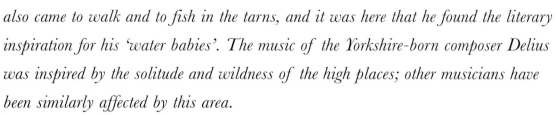

appropriate for his style of art. William and Dorothy Wordsworth were irresistibly drawn from their beloved Lake District, so close to the Dales; Charles Kingsley also came to walk and to fish in the tarns, and it was here that he found the literary inspiration for his 'water babies'. The music of the Yorkshire-born composer Delius was inspired by the solitude and wildness of the high places; other musicians have been similarly affected by this area.

The Dales themselves produced the pioneering geologist, Adam Sedgewick, and the Kearton brothers, Cherry and Richard, who were among the first to promote the

Victorian enthusiasm for natural history. They went to great lengths to obtain what were, at that time, unique and amazing photographs.

By the turn of this century the Yorkshire Dales had become a great focus of interest for the more adventurous: the walkers, climbers and pot-holers. The Yorkshire Ramblers' club had also been formed and had managed to climb all of the Three Peaks – Ingleborough, Penyghent and Whernside – in ten and a half hours, and the Frenchman E. A. Martel had made the first descent into the pot-hole Gaping Gill.

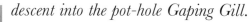

In 1954, 680 square miles of mainly privately owned land in the Yorkshire Dales were designated a National Park, and visitors came, encouraged by the veterinary surgeon and author Alf Wight, better known as James Herriott. His books and televised stories made the Yorkshire Dales familiar to people worldwide. J. B. Priestley and Howard Spring set novels here and film-makers frequently come, anxious to use the dramatic scenery as a backdrop.

However, this unique and beautiful landscape does not suffer from the surfeit of tourists that can afflict the Lake District and the West Country. Even in high summer, one does not have to venture far to enjoy pleasant riverside walks by meadows thick with wildflowers, cool rushing waterfalls and the wonderful aerial vistas, all in perfect solitude.

This magical scenery is set in a farming landscape, which belongs to the descendants of the tough and resilient people who have settled here throughout the centuries. As they go about their daily work, these no-nonsense Dalesmen and -women are always ready to offer a friendly welcome to the jaded urban dwellers who come to experience the magic and mystery of the glorious Yorkshire Dales.

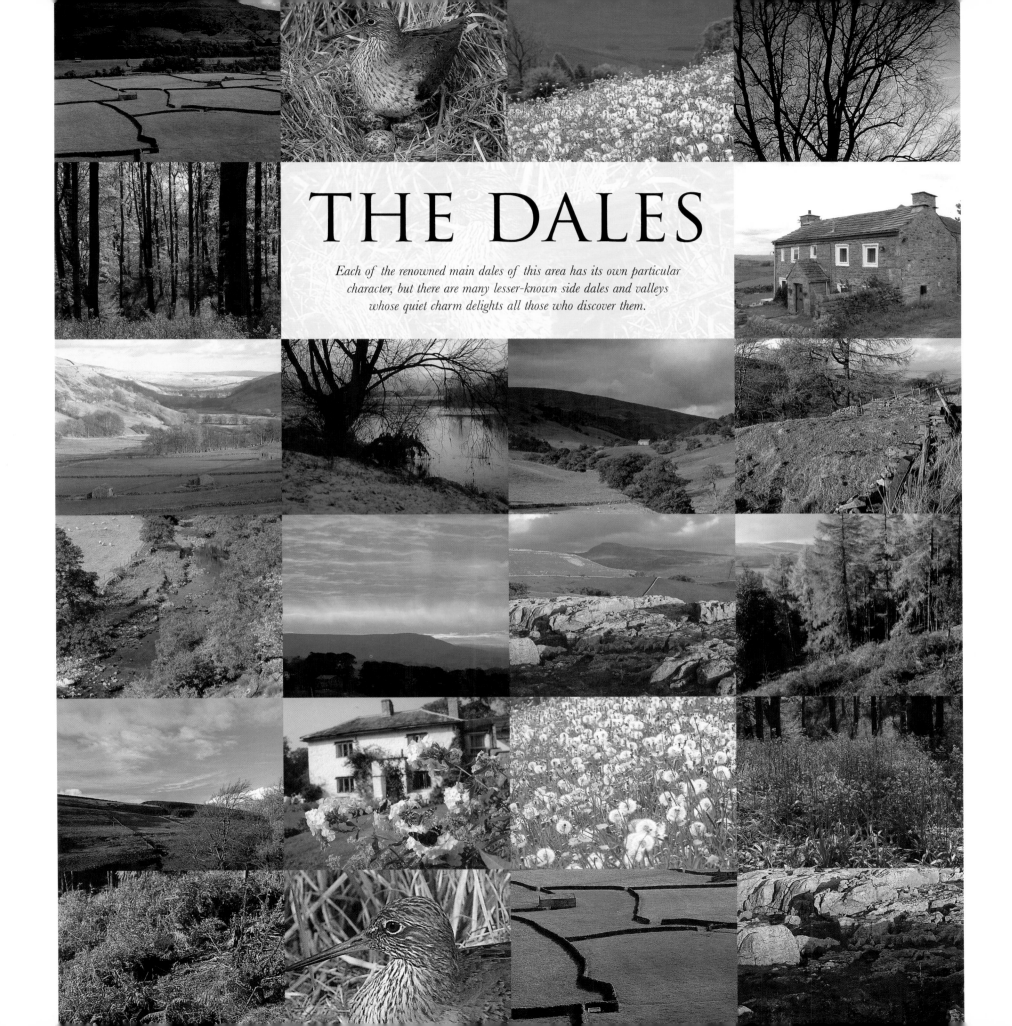

THE DALES

Each of the renowned main dales of this area has its own particular character, but there are many lesser-known side dales and valleys whose quiet charm delights all those who discover them.

Swaledale Barns and Walls
NEAR GUNNERSIDE

The River Swale, the most northerly of the Dales rivers, meanders swiftly through a fertile valley which displays so many of the features that are the magic of the Yorkshire Dales. From the tiny cluster of cottages at Keld, with its waterfalls, to the elegant town of Richmond this rugged dale is a joy.

Ancient tracks run across the land, and miles of dry stone walls thread their way up the steep hillsides, dotted with many stone barns. Flanking the sinuous curves of the river, lush hay meadows flourish, for this is a pastoral landscape, and the hay provides winter feed for the animals, including the hardy, black-faced Swaledale sheep.

Pretty villages are strung out along the dale, and once housed the families of the miners during the height of lead production when, it is said, Swaledale lead was used for the roof of the Vatican.

As the river flows eastwards, the villages begin to take on a more prosperous aspect, and Bede's 'Rushing River' swirls triumphantly below the elegance and sophistication of Richmond, and on into the Vale of York.

Walden Valley
BISHOPDALE

The Walden valley is one of the 'secret' dales, for it is a side dale of Bishopdale, itself one of Wensleydale's larger tributary valleys.

At its lower end, where Walden Beck tumbles over small waterfalls, is the lovely village of West Burton, and at its head the road forks to run up either side of the stream. However, both of these roads end abruptly on the moorland and the valley runs up to Walden Head below towering Buckden Pike. It is this 'cul-de-sac' feature and lack of a through road which has ensured the preservation of the quiet and timeless air of this lovely valley.

Woodland flanks the stream and there is hardly any human intrusion, only the sheep which dot the hillsides and moorland, and on the lower pastures the cows grazing placidly.

This is an idyllic scene which has hardly changed for generations, and is one of the greatest delights of the Dales.

Langstrothdale Chase from Hubberholme
UPPER WHARFEDALE

Above the village of Hubberholme there is an extensive platform of limestone pavements which gives an unsurpassed view up the length of Wharfedale, showing the characteristic 'U'-shaped glacial valley, and to the right of this vantage point, a long, heavily wooded dale can be seen.

Langstrothdale is a beautiful and unfrequented tributary valley, which joins Wharfedale just to the north of Buckden, and the Chase was once a hunting preserve of the Norman Lords of Skipton. Fountains Abbey once owned the dale and its many outlying granges here, where their flocks of sheep were tended. On Cam Moor above this remote valley, the rivers Wharfe and Ribble are born, and the road which runs through Langstrothdale Chase becomes the moorland track of the Pennine Way. On Fleet Moss Moor, the herring-bone pattern of open ditches can be seen, and at the upper end of the dale, new conifer plantations are growing on pastures where the first experiments with lime and its benefit to crops were carried out in 1774.

Woodland
WHARFEDALE

The River Wharfe rises in the Askrigg block on Cam Fell, and at its small beginnings as a mountain stream it scampers down pretty little gills or ravines, and by limestone pavements and caves. The tributary valleys of Littondale and Langstrothdale add their own magic to Wharfedale and its bewitching and varied landscape.

The wild and lonely moors roll out above this broad glaciated valley, with its luxuriant meadows and pretty villages strung out along the river. From its source the Wharfe is always fast moving, its meandering passage is deceptive and it can be treacherous. At one stage, it hurls itself through a narrow wooded ravine with such fury that it changes its name. Here, where many have lost their lives, it is known as the Strid.

The river is subject to sudden rises in its levels and the bridges which span it are strongly fortified for they replace many others which have been swept away by the river in spate.

Evening
LITTONDALE

The setting sun casts a glow over one of the lovely tributary valleys of Wharfedale. Littondale has seen much of the history of the Yorkshire Dales and shadows cast by the lowering sun bring the medieval farming terraces, or lynchets into sharp relief on the slopes. The Norman aristocracy hunted here, and old tracks lead on to Settle and cross the high ridge into Wharfedale. Litton village, which gives its name to the dale, is situated in the shadow of Darnbrook Fell, to the eastern side of Fountains Fell, where shallow depressions indicate that coal was once mined here.

Littondale's best known village is Arncliffe. Surrounded by sloping moorland it is situated on a well-drained bed of gravel, which raises it above the dampness of the flat valley floor, its limewashed houses surrounding a pretty green. Charles Kingsley stayed here and Littondale was the model for Vendale in his story of *The Water Babies*.

Beside the River Skirfare stands the church of St Oswald's where the names of Littondale men who fought at the Battle of Flodden Field in 1513 can be seen – names still found in the dale today.

Sunset
RIBBLESDALE

The River Ribble is the only main dale river to run westwards from the Pennine watershed, and its dale is also exceptional for its geology. Ribblesdale displays all the extraordinary features of typical karst scenery, where sudden underground drainage occurs in a limestone landscape. This results in dry valleys, caves, pot-holes and sink holes, and the biggest and most impressive in the country can be found along the Ribble's course.

Where Fell Beck drains into Ingleborough's Gaping Gill, it disappears to plunge 340 feet. This famous pot-hole is reputed to be spacious enough to hold York Minster. Hull Pot on Penyghent is another mighty chasm where heavy rainfall causes a cascade of water which is swallowed up and disappears.

In Ribblesdale these vanishing watercourses eventually surface again from many famous caves which are often long distances from the swallow holes. The water tumbling into Gaping Gill flows out at the capacious White Scar Cave, which is a great attraction in itself, for its roof is hung with a mesmerising number of stalactites.

After it has rolled through this memorable landscape the Ribble continues its westerly journey; it is the only Dales river to flow into the Irish sea.

Great Coume
DENTDALE

On the slopes of Great Coume to the south of Dent village, wildflowers grow in glorious profusion, just one of the splendours of this very beautiful dale. Gentle green slopes rise on either side of the River Dee, feeding it with a host of small streams and becks that drain their heights. The valley is dotted with whitewashed farmhouses and the stone walls which lace their way across the eastern dales are replaced here by trees and hedgerows.

There are signs of quarrying in Dentdale as the Victorian penchant for everything black, and the fashionable interest in geology, led to the great popularity of Dent marble. This is not really marble, just a very dark form of limestone, but it can be polished to an attractive gloss which reveals the white outline of its fossils. The quarrying of this highly prized rock became an important industry, and the Mill at Arten Gill was converted for the cutting of the limestone 'marble'. Unfortunately, the prosperity that this brought did not last, and the importing of cheaper Italian marble sounded the death knell of the industry, which was finished by the end of the last century.

Woodland Scene
NIDDERDALE

Nidderdale is the shortest of the main dales and the river Nidd drains into the Ouse and the Humber estuary, as do the Swale, Ure, Wharfe and Aire.

Upper Nidderdale is a wonderful moorland wilderness, providing challenging and exhilarating country for serious walkers. There are two great reservoirs in this area and the utilitarian nature of these 'lakes', which provided Bradford's water, was part of the reason for Nidderdale's exclusion from the National Park. However, as part of the Corporation Waterworks the public were kept away from the reservoirs. Thus they have been preserved, as unspoiled as if they had been protected as conservation areas.

The Nidderdale Way runs from Scar House reservoir and past the village of Middlesmoor on its astonishing perch. High on a ridge, it has the dramatic landscape of the steep ravine of the Nidd on one side, and How Stean Gorge on the other. The Nidd sweeps on past pretty woodland, and Gouthwaite reservoir which has become an important waterfowl preserve.

Beyond the dale's market town of Pateley Bridge, the landscape becomes more commonplace, but as so much of Nidderdale's scenery can equal the magnificence of the other Dales, one can only hope that the National Park's omission will be rectified.

Redshank
COVERDALE

In the quiet valley of Coverdale a redshank sits on her nest, well camouflaged by her plumage. These birds are waders and are generally found on open shoreland, where they feed on the small shellfish and lugworms of which they find plenty in the mud. They are year-round residents in this country and usually they gather in flocks, but during the breeding season pairs seek the seclusion of some damp corner, where they build a nest on the ground.

Coverdale has proved a favourite site, and the redshank is just one of the unusual birds which have discovered its peace and solitude. This tranquil and heavily wooded valley, Wensleydale's most southerly tributary valley, is a delight to discover. The River Cover joins the Ure at East Witton, and the unfrequented road that runs the length of the dale was an important packhorse trail, linking Wensleydale with Wharfedale at Kettlewell. The village of Horsehouse, halfway along the dale was the main resting place for travellers before the steep climb up on to the moors.

The Setting Sun
WENSLEYDALE

Wensleydale derives its name from its old capital town of Wensley, but the population there was decimated by the plague in the 16th century, and Hawes and Leyburn are now the dale's most important towns.

The wide water meadows of Wensleydale spread out below the woodland on its gently sloping hillsides. This pastoral scenery differs markedly from the other dales, for here is dairy country, and cows grazing the lush herbs and grasses have produced the milk for Wensleydale cheese for hundreds of years.

Down the ages, people came to this dale to settle and they all left their imprint: neolithic caves, ancient earthworks, Roman roads and a fort, and many Norse names. 'Abbotside' demonstrates the links with Jervaulx Abbey which once owned much of the land here.

The Pennine Way, and many other roads and paths converge here in this lovely dale which is literally awash with splendid waterfalls. The memorable scenery has long enticed our poets and artists; indeed, Turner returned again and again to capture on canvas the beauty of this wonderful, light-filled dale.

Butterflies at Beck House
MALHAM, AIREDALE

Malham Beck is one of the prettiest in the Dales, babbling from the foot of the cliff at Malham Cove, and past Beck House with its ancient clapper bridge.

Above the cove is Malham Tarn, a rare upland lake, whose waters are held in the limestone by a bed of non-porous slate. The water flows out of the lake and disappears into sink holes above the cove, and it is often assumed that the little beck's appearance, issuing from a narrow slit below, marks the resurgence. However, the outflow from the tarn does not reappear until a point south of the village, known as Aire head. The drama of Malham Cove and Gordale Scar is a complete contrast to the lush dairy pastures and pretty villages to the south

The Aire has a comparatively short run within the Yorkshire Dales, and from its beginnings to Gargrave, its dale is commonly known as Malhamdale. It has some wonderful walking country, and the Pennine Way footpath follows the river closely.

Gargrave is situated on the Aire Gap. Travellers and transport have used this ancient pass through the 'Backbone of England' since time immemorial and here the sparkling Aire sweeps southeast to Skipton and out of the Dales.

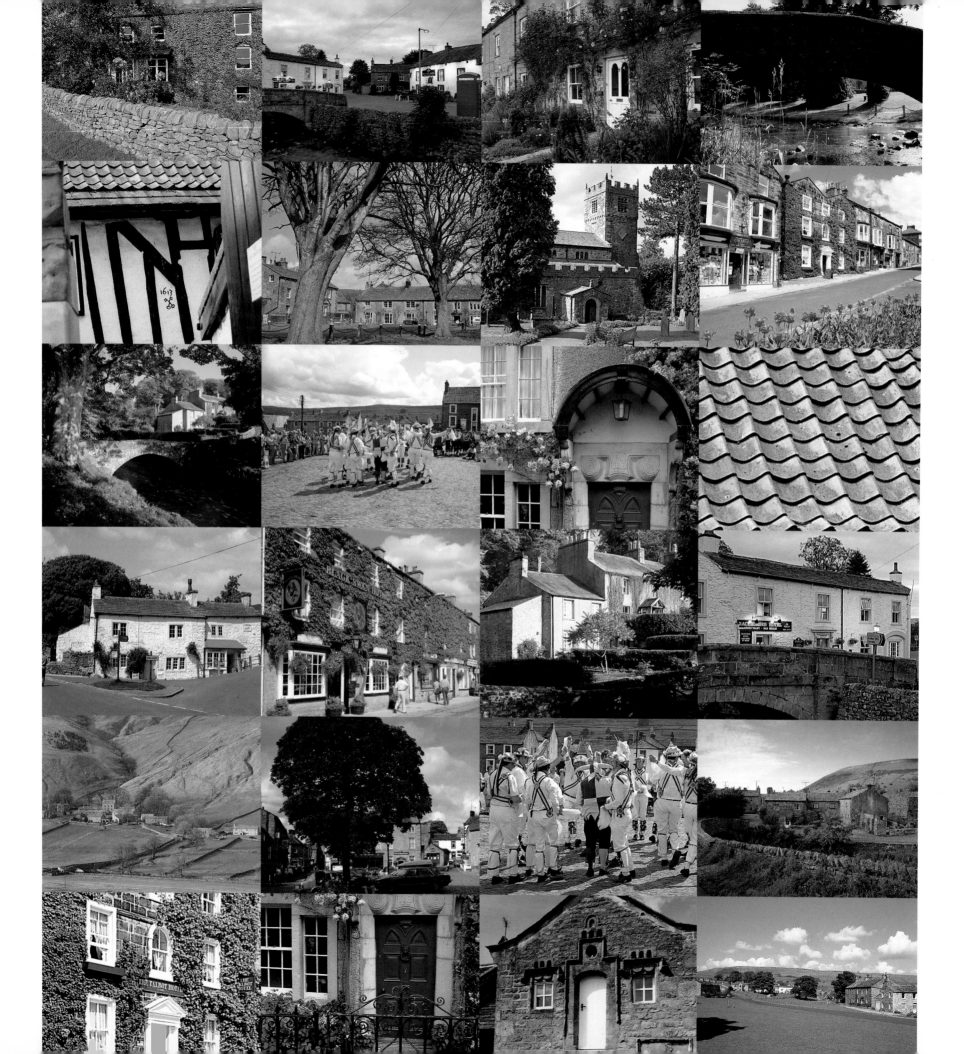

TOWNS & VILLAGES

Throughout the Dales, picturesque villages are legion. From whitewashed cottages to those built entirely of local stone, they blend with the glorious scenery, and the elegant larger towns retain the air of pleasant market towns.

Bainbridge
WENSLEYDALE

The houses and large green of Bainbridge are situated on both sides of what was once the main turnpike road running through Wensleydale. Most of the houses are about 200 years old, and at Low Mill corn milling took place until about 1920; after that time it became a dairy producing Wensleydale cheese. In 1947, during severe flooding, the river Bain burst through its dam and damaged the mill so severely that it could no longer be used. The Rose and Crown Inn was built in 1443, and in its hallway hangs the old curfew horn, which dates from the days when this community was a forest village.

Looking even further back in time, the Roman fort of Virosidium was built in AD 74 on the large drumlin which overlooks the village. It was perfectly situated on its hill which rises above the flat valley floor, overlooking both the Bain and the Ure. The road that the Romans built later became the turnpike road, and still runs on as straight as an arrow to Ingleton, continuing over Cam Fell as a track. Of the fort, only mounds and parts of the stone ramparts remain; a mere glimpse of how it looked when it housed a garrison of 500 men.

Malham Village

AIREDALE

This pretty village, with its limewashed cottages and outstandingly pretty beck, is host to all the visitors who come to marvel at the local limestone features of Malham Cove and Gordale Scar, and yet it remains utterly unspoilt.

Below its craggy geological formations, Malham village is set amongst Airedale's lush and gentle landscape of woods and pastures, where pleasant walks abound. The riverside path winds through flowery meadows, which hum with the sound of insects, and into Wedber Wood. Under its shady canopy is Janet's Foss, where water cascades over a large, green pillar of rock and tufa. Janet derives from the old name of Gennet, the name of a fairy queen who is thought to inhabit the cave behind the little waterfall, and certainly this pleasant little wood, where the young River Aire seems to whisper and chatter as it hurries over mossy rocks and pebbles, has all the qualities of a fairy dell.

Clapham Village
NEAR INGLEBOROUGH

The charming little village of Clapham is a rarity in the Dales, for it is full of trees. Tucked away in a thickly wooded valley, south east of Ingleborough, the cottages are built on either side of tree-lined Clapham Beck, and the village has no less than four bridges spanning its stream. Some of the picturesque waterfalls generate hydroelectric power for the grey stone houses, which are mostly 18th century. The church of St James is mainly Regency although it still retains its 12th-century tower.

Clapham is where the renowned Yorkshire Dalesman magazine has been published since 1939, although it has now been re-named The Dalesman. Another claim to fame is that Michael Faraday, the pioneer of modern electricity, was the son of the village Blacksmith.

Much of the village was owned by the Farrer family. Reginald Farrer was a distinguished botanist who became an authority on alpine flowers, and introduced very many new plants, earning him the title 'The Father of Rock Gardening'. There is some splendid walking country in the area, and Farrer has been commemorated with a nature trail leading through the private Ingleborough Estate with its lovely landscaped gardens, to the mouth of Ingleborough cave.

Thwaite
SWALEDALE

The cottages in the small village of Thwaite huddle together at the foot of Kisdon Hill, in the upper reaches of Swaledale. The pretty bridge and all the houses are built entirely of the local stone, blending harmoniously with the barns and walls which characterise this part of the dale.

Norsemen made their home in Thwaite, giving it a name which means 'clearing in a wood', suggesting that a forest probably flourished here before the land was cleared for farming. However, this isolated part of the dales was not settled to any great extent until a new wave of colonisers moved in, seeking suitable land for grazing their animals.

In the last century, this village was a lively place, for the men who mined the lead in Swaledale occupied the cottages. But then, in 1899 a tragic event occurred; a torrential flood swept down Thwaite Beck and engulfed the village, drowning almost every soul. The volume of water that poured through must have been enormous, for it is said that flowers uprooted from Thwaite were later found growing along the valley at the next village of Muker.

Sedbergh
GARSDALE

Sedbergh's church of St Andrew retains many original Norman features, although there are some 14th-century additions. It remains a venerable building, with old pews and alms boxes which add to the evocative atmosphere of centuries of history.

Nearby is the tiny marketplace where a market has been held since a charter was granted in 1251, but the old cross which once stood here was removed in 1897 and can now be found in the garden of the Quaker meeting house in Brigflatts. Some of the cobbled main street of Sedbergh has been designated a conservation area, and behind some splendid old houses are quaint alleyways and courtyards dating from Tudor times. There is also a 17th-century chimney breast, where Bonnie Prince Charlie is said to have hidden.

Sedbergh School was founded in 1525 by Roger Lupton and is now a famous public school. William Wordsworth sent his son John here, and Hartley Coleridge, the son of the poet, was a teacher here – until he was dismissed for drunkenness.

Burnsall
WHARFEDALE

Burnsall village lies in a glorious position on the River Wharfe. Its long bridge stretches gracefully from the grassy riverbanks and is sturdy enough to withstand the vagaries of the waters, which can rise alarmingly high. The bridge was bestowed in 1612 by William Craven who also endowed the grammar school (now a primary school). He was a local boy who made his fortune in London and became Lord Mayor from 1610 to 1612. On his return to the Dales he became a great benefactor.

The houses are all made of the local gritstone, a material usually reserved for lintels and cornerstones in the Dales. St Wilfred's church rises strikingly against the green hillside above the village and bridge. It has a Norman font and the churchyard contains some Anglo Norse gravestones. The Lychgate on the pretty village green is unusual as it is combined with the village stocks.

The lovely scenery makes this an ideal starting point for many long walks. One of the riverside paths leads to a little suspension bridge and a footpath to Hebden, providing access to the outstandingly beautiful surrounding countryside, with its woodland, moorland and pleasant pastures.

Dent Village
DENTDALE

Dent is a true picture-postcard village of whitewashed cottages, with dark sandstone roofs and twisting cobbled streets surrounded by verdant scenery. It also has the highest railway station in Britain, which stands at a height of 1,150 feet. Surprisingly, it is five miles from the village.

There is a granite fountain in the main street, placed here as a memorial to Adam Sedgewick, the local man who became a pioneer geologist, and the solid bulk of Saint Andrew's church can be seen rising above the village. It is a large building which was rebuilt in Victorian times, but it retains its Norman doorway and has a very attractive interior. The chancel floor is paved with shining Dent marble and there are some Jacobean box pews.

Dent was the hub of the hand-knitting industry – which once flourished in the Dales. People would come here to learn the craft, and women would gather to sing and knit in each others' homes; there were 'knitting galleries' in many of the houses. Today, there are still accomplished knitters here, as well as a thriving artistic community of craft workers, whose work is much sought after by the village's many tourists.

Halton Gill
LITTONDALE

Far up in the wilds of Upper Littondale, beyond the place where the beck-draining Penyghent meets the Skirfare, the tiny village of Halton Gill nestles into the undulating folds of the landscape. Viewed from the height of the Stainforth road the hamlet's isolation is starkly apparent, for the lonely moors roll away endlessly, entirely devoid of any other sign of habitation.

Most of Halton Gill's houses and farms, all of which cluster picturesquely around a small green, date back to the 17th century. In the days when the packhorse trails brought frequent travellers through this village it was a lively place, but now this is the most isolated village in the Dales.

Two miles higher up is the even lonelier farmhouse of Cosh House – the most remote single dwelling. Inaccessibility is an integral feature of this rugged countryside and frequently means loneliness and isolation. Often this has led to desolation and decay, as inhabitants of solitary farms and cottages have sought companionship in the more accessible areas, leaving the buildings to crumble away.

Whole villages have gone too and the only evidence of their existence, that still remains today, is the faintly discernible shapes in the land that they once occupied.

GRASSINGTON
WHARFEDALE

The pretty and quaint village of Grassington is, justifiably, a very popular tourist centre, yet it remains quite unspoilt. It retains all the charm of former, less hurried times, with Georgian houses and cottages surrounding its cobbled square, and lining its narrow sloping streets. Amongst the older cottages is the home of one Tom Lee who, in 1766, murdered the local doctor and threw the body into the Wharfe. Lee was hanged in York. The museum on the square has an absorbing display showing the history of farming and industry in Upper Wharfedale.

The discovery of lead on the nearby moors led to an increase in population and prosperity, and Grassington became a very lively place. This was tempered by John Wesley's visit here on his preaching tour (a plaque on 'Wesley's Barn' dated 1783 commemorates this trip). He had a sobering influence on the miners' notoriously wild ways, which had previously brought the village into disrepute.

Grassington today is a peaceful and pleasant place, surrounded by enchanting riverside walks, pretty waterfalls and cool woodlands.

Muker
SWALEDALE

Muker was originally a Norse settlement, but plentiful evidence of neolithic settlements has been discovered close to the village. It is the biggest of the unpretentious villages of Upper Swaledale, which lie strung out alongside the River Swale as it snakes along the valley.

The church stands high, set against the hillside, and has Elizabethan origins although Victorian embellishments and additions are more evident now. Built in 1580 it was a chapel of ease where coffin bearers would stop to rest before continuing their journey to the church at Grinton, and Queens Inn used to keep tankards especially for these coffin carriers.

There is a plaque in the church which commemorates Richard and Cherry Kearton who went to the school here and whose wildlife books and early photographs were received with such great acclaim. It was on Muker Moor that Richard met Sidney Galpin of Cassells publishing house, and the position he took up there provided the springboard for his distinguished career as a writer and lecturer.

Each September, the Muker Show takes place. Farmers and stockbreeders flock here, along with the general public, to see the animals being judged and to take part in the sporting events.

Kettlewell
WHARFEDALE

Evening descends on the tranquil village of Kettlewell and its bridge. The water flowing beneath the bridge bequeathed the town its Norse name, which means 'bubbling spring'. Kettlewell is the capital of Upper Wharfedale and grew in importance in the 13th century when it was given a market charter. Much of the land surrounding the village was once owned by Bolton Priory and the abbeys of Fountains and Coverham, and the many roads that led here are still to be seen. Later, the establishment of the important lead mining centre to the south of Kettlewell at Grassington, and the development of the local textile industry, led to most of the 17th- and 18th-century houses being built. The church was added in Victorian times. There is a story that relates how one impoverished parson turned his house into an inn to supplement his income.

Kettlewell is situated in the most magnificent part of Wharfedale. Watched over by the bulk of Great Whernside and its limestone scars, the village lies quietly surrounded by Celtic fields and the picturesque lines of drystone walls which shoot up the green hillsides.

Hawes
WENSLEYDALE

When approaching Hawes along the Pennine Way, one's first view is of the pointed steeple of the Victorian church, followed by the rest of this bustling little town. St Margaret's church has a light and pleasant oak furnished interior, and was built in just one year (in 1850), at a cost of only £3,000.

The name 'Hawes' is derived from 'Hals' – a Norse word meaning 'neck' – indicative of the town's site between two ranges of hills. At 850 feet above sea level it is one of the highest market towns, and one of the most important in the Yorkshire Dales. Despite its popularity with tourists, Hawes exudes an old fashioned charm, with its busy weekly market, attractive houses and local craftsmen.

Perfectly situated in Upper Wensleydale there is easy access from the town to many rewarding walks, and a drive across Wether Fell and Fleet Moss Pass – at a height of 1,857 feet – offers truly breathtaking views.

With the coming of the railway in 1877, Hawes became established as the capital of Wensleydale, and in 1897 the cheese factory was opened. The rail link is gone, but the creamery continues to produce fine Wensleydale cheeses and draws crowds of visitors who come to see it being made.

Cottage in Thoralby

BISHOPDALE

One of Wensleydale's least known tributary valleys is Bishopdale, and Thoralby is one of its secret treasures. Hidden away from the Wharfedale road and close to Bishopdale Beck, it has an old mill and waterfall, and is set amidst delightfully varied scenery. Near the small village green is an ancient pinfold (an enclosure for cattle), and the houses which radiate away from it are mainly 18th century. The few modern houses blend in sympathetically. The old village paths lead to the other Bishopdale villages and into Aysgarth with its waterfalls.

The village commands a splendid view of Burton Moor and the high white

gash of Dove Scar on the opposite side of the dale; grassy slopes rise up behind it leading to Thoralby moor. Cattle grazing in the meadows around Thoralby and flanking the beck, are an indication of its proximity to Wensleydale.

A walk through Thieves' Gill threads attractively through a scatter of large grassy mounds. These are drumlins; smooth lumps of boulder clay which were dropped and shaped by the Bishopdale glacier, and their distinctive 'basket of eggs' pattern can be seen all about the valley floor.

Cottages at Marske
SWALEDALE

Marske in Swaledale is a charming little village situated well away from the main road into Richmond, hidden amongst the farmland and richly wooded hills of a small tributary valley.

On a slope above Marske Beck, the little Norman church sits between the pretty rose-covered cottages of the village. St Edmund's dates from 1090 and still retains some of its original features, including the Norman door arches. This was once a forest village, and the valley was a Norman hunting chase – on the stone arch of the church's south doorway are the scratches and grooves where swords and arrows were sharpened.

There are later additions to this tiny church, dating from the 14th, 17th and 19th centuries. All the seating is in box pews which were put in by John Hutton of Marske Hall in 1823 – the pews reside respectfully over the graves of Hutton's father and grandfather. The church and its village have had close associations with Marske Hall ever since Matthew Hutton, the then Archbishop of York, acquired it in 1597. This graceful and well-proportioned house is situated amongst sloping lawns and ornamental gardens which spread up to the perimeter of the village.

Pateley Bridge
NIDDERDALE

Nidderdale does not lie within the Yorkshire Dales National Park area, but it is nevertheless one of the major dales. In contrast with other Dales villages, Pateley Bridge has a rather striking aspect, for its 18th- and 19th-century houses are built with the dark local gritstone. The medieval church was abandoned in 1827 for St Cuthbert's. When John Wesley came here on his tour of the north, the vicar allowed him to use the medieval church which was much larger than Wesley's preaching house. Wesley noted 'but it was not near large enough to contain our congregation'.

The village was granted a market charter in the 14th century and had an important position on the trading route from the Craven area to Fountains Abbey and Ripon. When steam replaced water power for the textile industry in the 19th century, the village's prosperity declined.

Pateley has also become renowned for its Folk Museum: an old Victorian warehouse housing a fascinating display in eleven rooms. It won the Natural Heritage Museum of the Year award in 1990.

Morris Men
REETH, SWALEDALE

Morris dancing is a ritual folk dancing tradition whose origins are uncertain but thought to derive from Moorish dance. The dancers are clad in white and wear bells. They often paint their faces, usually carry sticks and white handkerchiefs, and perform dances symbolic of various themes and rituals, many of which involve fertility.

These modern Morris Men are dancing on the large triangular green at Reeth, surrounded by its three-storey shops, and sprawl of 18th- and 19th-century houses and hotels. Reeth is much bigger than the other villages further up Swaledale, owing its more prosperous air to its lead mining history.

A huge weekly market used to be held here, when an amazing array of goods would be spread out on the green: clogs, ironmongery, meat and clothes were sold, and it was said that anything could be bought here 'from a pin to a pig'.

The Swaledale Folk Museum houses a fascinating and informative collection, showing the history of the dale – including lead mining, farming, village life and religion – and is very popular with the many visitors who flock here, also to stroll about the large, airy green and enjoy the wonderful wide view of the moors.

Leyburn
WENSLEYDALE

The name of Leyburn is derived from Le Borne, and is mentioned in the Domesday Book; this high market town is now the principal administrative centre for Wensleydale. It owes its importance to the depopulation of nearby Wensley, during the plague of 1563, and to the Lords of Bolton Castle who ensured that the town received its market charter, albeit rather late, in 1684. Later, with the coming of the railway linking the town to Garsdale and the Settle to Carlisle line, Leyburn's continuing prosperity was ensured.

This is a very attractive town with inns, houses and shops surrounding a wide market place, where a busy weekly market is held. A short walk from the centre is Thornborough Hall, a large elegant building which houses the administration offices and the Tourist Information Centre. It was once the home of the Catholic Thornborough family, and the priest hole and secret cellars still exist as a reminder of the days when the performing of Catholic mass was forbidden.

Linton-in-Craven
WHARFEDALE

Linton-in-Craven is one of the most delightful villages in the Dales, apparently undisturbed by the passage of time. A small beck babbles below a sloping green, overlooked by the 17th- and 18th-century limestone houses and Fountaines Hospital. This row of six almshouses with its surprisingly impressive facade, was founded by Richard Fountaine. Born in Linton in 1639, he made his fortune in London, selling timber after the Great Fire. The hospital dominates the village with its grand Palladian style, and is generally ascribed to Sir John Vanbrugh, the architect of Castle Howard. Originally intended for poor men of the parish, it is still in use and now treats both men and women.

There is a Victorian bridge across Linton's beck, a 14th-century packhorse bridge, and an ancient clapper bridge. A ford and stepping stones ensure that the visitor has an abundance of ways to reach the little pub which nestles amongst the trees on the far side.

St Michael's is Linton's church, although it is some distance from the village. It stands picturesquely alone on the banks of the river Wharfe, and close to the tumbling waters of the shallow Linton Falls.

Settle
RIBBLESDALE

Beneath the towering crags of Warrendale Knotts and Attermire Scar, Settle is situated at the Aire Gap and is the gateway to the South Western Dales. It owed its importance initially to the traffic which came through here, and its further prosperity to the coming of the railway and the Settle to Carlisle line in 1876.

This very pleasant little town has consistently held a weekly market in its square for almost 750 years. On the market square stands a house with a plaque which proclaims that Elgar stayed here on his frequent visits to his friend Dr Buck, and on the site of the old open market is an arcade of shops, still known as The Shambles.

A Victorian fountain replaced the old market cross and it stands before an oddly named cafe; 'Ye Olde Naked Man'. This cafe was formerly an inn, and the name is a satirical comment on the elaborate fashions which once prevailed. The 'Old Naked Woman' can be found in Langcliffe.

Appropriately, the remains of the first settlers in the Yorkshire Dales have been found near Settle, in Victoria Cave, so named because it was discovered on Queen Victoria's Jubilee Day.

Mock Beggar Hall
APPLETREEWICK

Appletreewick is pronounced 'Aptrick' locally, and means 'dairy farm near apple tree'. This is a very pretty, one-street village, built on a slope which allows an unrestricted view of the magnificent countryside.

Despite being so small, Appletreewick has some notable houses dating from the 15th and 16th centuries. Low Hall is situated at the bottom of the street, and High Hall, at the top, was the home of William Craven, the great Dales benefactor. Having left his home town, he travelled by cart to London where he began his working life in a drapers shop – incredibly he went on to become Lord Mayor. When he returned, Craven restored the house which has three storeys and once had a two-storey porch.

The village was granted a market charter in 1311, raising it to the status of a town. This enabled the villagers to hold their 'Onion Fair.' The green track known as Onion Lane leads down to the banks of the Wharfe, where strings of onions were once sold.

Mock Beggar Hall, was once known as Monks' Hall. The village came under the ownership of Bolton Priory and this is the site of a monastic grange.

Old Courthouse
RIPON

Dwarfed by the glory of the cathedral's soaring west front, the old courthouse of Ripon shelters within a walled courtyard. In 886, the 'Liberty of Ripon' was granted by King Alfred the Great, this made Ripon independent of the West Riding of Yorkshire. The town's market charter was bestowed at around the same time. Because of this separate jurisdiction, the town required its own gaolhouse – in the 18th century, the old courthouse filled this post.

In 1836, when Ripon Minster became a Cathedral, Ripon became the smallest city in Yorkshire; however it still retains all the atmosphere of an old market town. This is a popular town with tourists, and the remarkable Law and Order Museums are a focus of great interest. The Prison and Police Museum in St Marygate provides us with a grim reminder of law enforcement in days gone by and there is a vast collection of police memorabilia including stocks, pillories and whipping posts.

The medieval town was centred around the cathedral and market square, but today the attractive houses are mainly Georgian and Victorian. The old Wakeman's house is a 16th-century, half-timbered building, where the last Wakeman, Hugh Ripley lived. The Wakeman was the town's hornblower, and the custom of sounding the curfew at each corner of the square, every evening at nine o'clock, continues to this day.

WATERFALLS,
RIVERS & LAKES

*Everywhere within the Dales the sound of water is heard, splashing over
rocks, rushing through narrow ravines or thundering into deep pools.
Here can be found Britain's biggest falls and cataracts.*

Hardraw Force
NEAR HAWES

At 96 feet Hardraw Force is the highest single drop cataract in England, and J.M.W. Turner came here to paint his Hardraw Falls, which shows the waterfall as an awesome torrent.

After heavy rainfall at its source on Abbotside Common, the Force is a spectacular sight, and the loud booming of the water as it drops into the pool below is strikingly amplified by the curve and overhanging rocks of this natural auditorium. During drier spells the water diminishes, and it is possible to walk behind the curtain of water where a recess has been carved out.

As well as beauty, Nature has also provided excellent acoustics and these have led to concerts being held here. For over one hundred years very popular annual brass band contests have also been held here.

Situated just a mile north of Hawes, the Force is reached via the Green Dragon Inn which exacts a small toll for access. An inn has been here for 750 years, although the toll bridge was probably the idea of an enterprising Victorian landlord. At that time, people would flock here to enjoy such spectacles as the famous acrobat Blondin, walking across the gorge on a tightrope. He even paused to fry some eggs when he was halfway across!

Upper Aysgarth Falls
WENSLEYDALE

The triple waterfalls at Aysgarth form a renowned beauty spot, and the very wide, shallow steps of the Upper Falls, make this one of the Yorkshire Dales' greatest attractions. People come to picnic in the waterside meadow and frolic in the many small cascades.

Middle Falls and Lower Falls drop more steeply through a narrower part of the limestone gorge below the bridge and the old Yore Mill. The mill was originally built in 1784 for spinning worsted yarn, and was completely destroyed by fire in 1853. Rebuilt a year later it produced 7,000 red shirts for General Garibaldi's volunteers.

There are nature trails in Freeholders Wood, and wooden platforms have been erected to allow splendid, unobstructed views of these falls. This pretty woodland, with its coppiced hazels, lines one bank of the Lower Falls and is a haven for wildlife. It is just a small fragment of the great forest which once filled Wensleydale, and although this comes under the management of the National Parks Authority, it is still a wood which belongs to local people, and they retain the ancient right to gather free firewood.

The Strid
WHARFEDALE

Close to Bolton Priory, the River Wharfe changes its pace and its name; it becomes The Strid and makes a headlong rush through a narrow and infamous gritstone gorge. Between its banks the water boils where pebbles of sandstone and bright, white quartz have swirled ceaselessly, wearing and enlarging the pot-holes that have been scooped in the hard rocks over ages.

At one point the ravine narrows to only four feet, and green mossy rocks reach out from either bank to hang over the torrent mid-stream. Many people have been tempted to leap across this treacherous gap, and have lost their lives in the dark and swiftly flowing river, which reaches a depth of 30 feet in places. Visitors today are warned that anyone who falls into the water here is not liable to surface for three days!

On either side of the ravine lie the 130 acres of Strid Woods; a site of 'Special Scientific Interest'. Along the marked nature trails beneath the beech, oak and sycamores, the green floor of the woodland is filled with wild flowers, and the air rings with the voices of the multitude of birds who come to nest here.

Birkdale Beck
NEAR KELD

Birkdale Beck mingles its water with those of the many little streams that tumble amongst the heather on Birkdale Moor; as they run past Keld the waters become the river Swale.

This is how the main rivers of the Dales begin, high on the Pennine watershed amongst the millstone grit and heather, or the sandstones where the water bubbles up from the mossy peat. Particularly after heavy rainfall in the hills, these boggy origins colour the clear waters of many of the rivers and streams with brown, and tint the weirs and waterfalls with gold.

The swift running waterways of the Dales are almost entirely unpolluted, and fish swim in most of the bigger streams and pools. In the dark basin below Janet's

Foss large fish can be seen leaping, and on the riverbanks people fish for trout, roach and grayling. The fish play an important part in the life cycle of the valleys, supporting colonies of mink and sometimes the rare otter. The ubiquitous heron fishes in the shallows, and sand martins and dippers feed on the insects, sweeping and darting over the waters.

Beezley Falls
INGLETON

Below the heights of Kingsdale, the River Doe flows down to the deep ravine that makes up one half of the Ingleton waterfalls area, and Beezley Falls is the first cascade of its tumultuous descent.

This spectacular series of waterfalls was not discovered until the 19th century. It was first opened to the public in 1885 – within three years the number of daily visitors exceeded 4,000, all paying a penny entrance fee.

The path that leads through the classic 'Waterfalls Walk' runs through excellent primary woodland, which is a valuable, although sadly diminishing wildlife habitat; it is the last bastion of the red squirrel in the Dales. Tawny owls and woodpeckers can be heard and little wrens and dippers dart about close to the thundering falls; in the craggy surface of the limestone, fungus and lichen flourish, revelling in the damp conditions.

Nestling at the foot of Ingleborough, the village of Ingleton is surrounded by a wealth of dramatic geological scenery, and is dominated by the 11-arched railway viaduct. Built in 1860, it was this railway that carried the first excursion trains, bringing thousands of visitors. Although the line was closed in 1954, people still flock to the village.

Semer Water
NEAR BAINBRIDGE

The calm waters of Yorkshire's largest natural lake are a magnet for anyone who enjoys water sports. Boating enthusiasts flock to Semerwater in the summer, and the sailing vessels add to the charm of the scene. The occasional hardy swimmer can sometimes be spotted braving the chilly waters, but most visitors simply come to enjoy the delightful views.

The lake was formed when a terminal moraine of boulder clay dammed the waters of a melting glacier, and the lake once reached three miles up Raydale. It is now much smaller, being only half a mile long and having a circumference of under two miles – an easy stroll. There are traces of Iron Age people in the shallows of the lake where they built houses on stilts, and Neolithic flint arrowheads have also been found.

There are three villages around Semer Water. Near its head is Marsett, a farming community gathered about a green where cattle graze; Countersett, with its strong Quaker connections, is the closest to the lake and Stalling Busk is one of the highest villages in the dales. In a field nearby is the unusual and atmospheric ruin of a tiny chapel.

Stainforth Force
RIBBLESDALE

Stainforth Force races beneath wooded banks and cascades over limestone steps as it rushes to join the River Ribble. The waterfall and the deep dark pool it has created can be reached by a footpath leading from a bridge which spans the river. This packhorse bridge was built in about 1670 to replace the 'stony ford' which was part of an ancient drove road linking York and Lancaster, and gave Stainforth its name.

The pleasant village has some limewashed houses and a small green, where a footpath leads along the side of Stainforth Beck overlooked by Langliffe Scar. Below this rests 'Samson's Toe', a large dark erratic rock perched on a narrow pedestal, and similar to those found at Norber. Stainforth's hidden second waterfall is reached here. Catrigg Force hurtles through a narrow chasm, plunging 60 feet in all, and during the winter some spectacular ice formations develop. Closely surrounded by trees this presents a magical sight in this 'secret' Dales location.

ABBEYS & CASTLES

The Yorkshire Dales boast some of the most atmospheric, enchanting and complete ruined abbeys and castles in England. These historic remains are now preserved under the protection of the National Parks Authority.

Marrick Priory
SWALEDALE

The remains of Marrick Priory lie in seclusion, below the wooded slopes of Swaledale. Half a mile from Marrick village, the priory can be reached by a stone causeway known as the 'Nuns Steps'.

Not long after the Benedictine and Cistercian orders of monks came to the Yorkshire Dales, the nuns started to arrive, and in Swaledale two nunneries were built. The one at Ellerton no longer exists, but Marrick Priory's few remains can still be seen.

During the period of the Dissolution there was wholesale destruction of religious buildings but, unusually, this priory escaped. The nuns made a long and courageous stand which lasted for five years, until they were finally forced to leave.

There was no deliberate destruction of the priory and the building simply fell into decay through neglect, some parts later being incorporated into a nearby farmhouse. Although the priory tower was left untouched the church was completely rebuilt in 1811. The chapel is used as a field study centre now, but Marrick Priory is not open to the general public. However, this area is idyllic to visit and enjoy the peace and tranquillity which the women of the original priory must have found here so long ago.

Bolton Castle
WENSLEYDALE

Bolton Castle stands solidly four square, occupying a magnificent position high above Wensleydale. It was built in 1397 by Sir Richard Scrope, and as it was never expected to be used for defensive purpose he ensured that it had many domestic comforts. The Scropes were powerful aristocrats of Norman descent, and Sir Richard became an MP and Chancellor of the Exchequer. Scrope is pronounced Scroop and a character of this name who features in Shakespeare's Henry IV was probably a member of the family.

Mary, Queen of Scots was imprisoned here for almost two years, although imprisonment is hardly the correct term, for she brought a retinue of about 60 members of her household, and carts groaning with the weight of her possessions. The Castle was besieged by Cromwell's troops in 1645 and finally starved into submission. After the Civil War it remained unoccupied for more than 300 years.

Today it is being given a new lease of life by the present Lord Bolton. His main preoccupation currently, is the establishment of a parterre – or formal garden – immediately in front of the castle where there will be a rose garden, a walled herb garden, a maze and a vineyard.

Barden Tower
WHARFEDALE

Medieval Barden Tower was built by Lord Henry Clifford, who was called 'The Shepherd Lord'; as a child he lived in exile in Cumbria during the Wars of the Roses, and was raised with a shepherd's family.

Although he built Barden Tower as a hunting lodge, Lord Henry, who was a scholarly man, preferred to live here in Barden's pleasant situation by the Wharfe, rather than at Skipton Castle. In 1513 at the age of 60, Lord Henry led Craven men at the Battle of Flodden where they helped to rout the Scots, and the Clifford family still keeps the halberd which he carried into battle.

Lord Henry's descendant was Lady Anne Clifford, who spent much of her childhood here, and renovated Barden Tower along with many other buildings, after the Civil War.

This is a lovely part of Wharfedale but the river can rise dramatically quickly. The elegant Barden bridge is these days well bolstered to withstand tremendous floods, for in 1673 it was entirely swept away, along with six other bridges on the Wharfe.

The atmospheric ruins in their green and tranquil setting make a wonderful scene, and artists have always flocked here, most famously Turner and Girtin.

Bolton Priory
WHARFEDALE

Bolton Priory is often erroneously called Bolton Abbey, but was built as a priory for Augustinian canons, known as 'Black Canons'. They came to this idyllic spot on a bend of the river Wharfe after more than 30 years at Embsay. The priory was founded in 1151 by Alice de Romille; it took a hundred years to complete. A short distance further south there are the treacherous waters of the Strid, and there is a story that she had the priory established in memory of her son, whose life was claimed by the infamous torrent.

Many years later, Prior Moon was adding a west tower when the Dissolution of the Monasteries began. He attempted to bribe Henry VIII's lieutenant but failed, and the monks were evicted. The building fell into ruins, and some of the stones were taken to build local houses.

The chancel is open to the sky, but the nave survives as the parish church and the splendour of the east window remains. These romantic ruins set in an exquisite pastoral landscape of woods and parkland, have drawn some of our most famous artists to try to capture its essence on canvas.

Brough Castle
NEAR KIRKBY STEPHEN

Situated on a grassy hill, all that remains of Brough castle and its chequered history are the 12th-century keep and enclosure wall. Although it lies outside the Yorkshire Dales National Park, the castle is historically connected with the Dales through Lady Anne Clifford of Skipton Castle.

There was once a Norman fortress here, built in 1095 by William Rufus, the son of the Conqueror, on the northern part of the Roman fortress of Vertrae. The Scots destroyed it in 1174 but it was rebuilt 30 years later. It was inherited by Lady Anne Clifford in the 17th century.

Lady Anne is remembered as a philanthropist, who had a great interest in the common people of the Dales. This doughty lady, who grew up at Barden tower, became a legend for her endless and tireless travels on horseback, visiting the many castles which she owned. The Clifford family

suffered greatly during the Civil War, when the Parliamentarians confiscated their properties. After the war, Lady Anne set about a great rebuilding programme, for as well as Brough, she owned the castles at Skipton, Brougham, Appleby and Pendragon Castle at Mallerstang.

After her death, Brough was allowed to fall into ruins but these remains have now been declared a National Monument, and are being preserved for posterity.

Fountains Abbey
NEAR RIPON

Fountains Abbey lies resplendent on grassy banks beside the little river Skell, which joins the Ure at Ripon, three miles away. The abbey was founded by a group of thirteen Benedictine monks who had rejected what they perceived to be the soft lifestyle of their abbey in York, in favour of the rigours of the Cistercian order.

Surrounded by thorn bushes and living in the shelter of trees and rocks, the monks would certainly have found the harsh way of life that they sought. They set about clearing the land, and the building of their abbey was completed in 1132. Fountains Abbey became the wealthiest abbey in Britain, due mainly to its trade in wool. The monks bought enormous numbers of sheep and cattle, which grazed on its farms or 'granges' that were spread across the southern dales as far west as Lancashire. Evidence of the one million acres once owned by the abbey can still be seen in place names such as Fountains Fell near Malham.

Fountains Abbey was a victim of the Dissolution and eventually fell into decay, but the glorious remains of this once great monastery should hardly be called ruins – so much still stands to delight the eye.

Easby Abbey
NEAR RICHMOND

The extensive ruins of Easby Abbey stand on a grassy bank overlooking the River Swale about a mile from Richmond. It was built in 1152 for Premonstratensian canons, who were of a similar order to the Cistercians, and in the 14th century it came into the hands of the powerful Scrope family.

The abbey was first damaged by marauding Scots and suffered further in 1346, in attacks of vandalism perpetrated by English soldiers who were billeted here. Little is left of the monastic church, but the walls of the refectory built in 1300 still stand tall, displaying some beautiful windows. The gate house also remains. An ornamental screen which came from Easby Abbey, can be seen in Wensley church.

St Agatha's church at Easby is much older than the abbey and has a plaster cast of an eighth-century cross, the original is now in the British Museum. This is a marvellous example of Anglo-Saxon sculpture depicting Christ and the Apostles on the front, with animals on the back. This church also has some well preserved 13th-century paintings on the chancel wall, and a Norman font.

Richmond Castle
SWALEDALE

When William the Conqueror had finally crushed the rebellious north, he divided the confiscated lands between his followers, determined to put an end to insurrection. Earl Alan Rufus, built his castle in its dramatic position, on a towering crag which hangs high over the fast-flowing River Swale.

The castle dates from about 1080, and one of the oldest parts to be seen today is Scolland's Hall, named after the Earl's steward. This is the oldest surviving Great Hall in England. A century later the keep was built and still stands at 100 feet high. It gives a birds eye view of the surrounding countryside, essential at a time when this stronghold suffered frequent attacks from the Scots.

Troops were garrisoned here continuously until the early twentieth century. There is a legend that King Arthur and his knights are sleeping with their treasure somewhere below Richmond, and some soldiers with an interest in the treasure once persuaded their small drummer boy to go down into the old passages. Afraid of meeting Arthur's ghost, the soldiers stayed above ground, following the sound of the boy's drumbeat. Just outside the town the beating stopped abruptly and the boy was never seen again. King Arthur slumbers on.

Skipton Castle
AIREDALE

In 1138, William Fitzduncan, a nephew of the King of Scotland, attacked Skipton Castle; however he later fell in love with and married the Norman Alice de Romille, whose family owned the castle. Afterwards it saw peace for almost 500 years.

It became thereafter the property of the Clifford family, during whose occupancy the Civil War broke out, and Cromwell's troops laid siege to many castles. At Skipton, Sir John Mallory resisted all attempts to take over the castle for three years, and with 300 men. They were eventually starved into submission and it was not for five years that Lady Anne Clifford was able to return to her battered home.

She restored many of her castles in the area over the next 25 years, but many are again in ruins today. However, at Skipton, the imposing result of her dedicated work still stands in a perfect state of preservation: the word 'Desormais' set over the gate, and meaning 'Henceforth' was perhaps prophetic.

The busy market town which stands at the gates of the castle, was a settlement long before the Normans came – Bronze Age graves have been found here. Today it is a very busy market town, of interesting, cobbled back streets and a mixture of buildings, some dating from the 14th century.

Jervaulx Abbey
NEAR MIDDLEHAM

Founded in 1156, Jervaulx Abbey was home to monks of the Cistercian order for almost four centuries, and its remains lie here still, imbued with the peace and solitude which these men sought so long ago. In 1537 this abbey, like so many others at the time, fell victim to Henry VIII's Dissolution. Its Abbot, Adam Sedbar was hanged at Tyburn for his part in the revolt known as 'The Pilgrimage of Grace', his actions also brought exceptionally ferocious destruction on his abbey.

Although almost totally in ruins, the ground plans are clearly visible today and on the grassy floor of the chapter house its elegant pillars still stand. The splendour of the great dormitory wall with its lancet windows, and 'night stair', dominates the scattered fragments of this mellow ruin, where there are fifteen different mason's marks to be found. These worn stones strewn amongst the riot of shrubs and wildflowers, are a haunting testimony to the ancient way of life that was once followed here.

Jervaulx lacks the spectacle and grandeur of some other, more complete abbey ruins, but in this peaceful setting, surrounded by the outstanding countryside of the area, it offers a rare, romantic charm.

LANDSCAPES

The Dales has some of the most dramatic and interesting geological features of a glaciated, limestone landscape in Britain. It has drawn visitors from around the world for more than 200 years.

The Buttertubs
NEAR THWAITE

The 'Buttertubs' are a great cluster of gaping sink holes in Upper Swaledale where the water from the bogs of Great Shunner Fell drains into the limestone.

These sink holes can be seen on both sides of the 1,726-foot high mountain pass road that runs from Thwaite to Hawes in Wensleydale. From the heart-stopping heights there is an awesome and thrilling vista of the fells and along the length of Swaledale. Stopping places on the route allow access to the deepest shafts which are situated on the eastern side, however great care should be taken as the sheer walls plummet to a depth of up to 90 feet.

At one time, the people of Thwaite travelled to the weekly market in Hawes to sell their butter and cheese, and it is said that on the homeward journey over the pass, they would lower any unsold merchandise into the cool and shady depths of these shafts, by means of baskets and ropes. The highly perishable goods would thus be preserved until the outward journey the following week. This could be how the Buttertubs came to be named, although the moniker may originate more mundanely from the shape of the limestone columns which resemble old buttertubs.

Ingleborough Peak
RIBBLESDALE

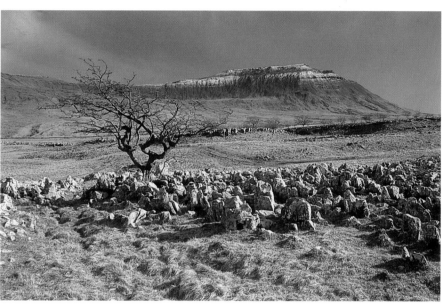

Ingleborough, rising majestically to a height of 2,373 feet, has some of the most impressive limestone features in the Dales. One of the famous 'Three Peaks', its height and astonishing variety of exciting caverns entice people from all over the world. Its distinctive tiers demonstrate the mixture of impervious and porous rocks, and it is the latter which has led to the formation of a multitude of pot-holes and caves. The most famous cave is named after the hill, and people have been coming here since it became a show cave in 1837. The legendary Gaping Gill has also drawn many intrepid pot-holers to explore its depths.

At Ingleborough's summit there are the remains of Britain's highest Iron Age fort, and close to this, ancient hut circles are evident. On the

northern point remain some intriguing stone walls of a house, which was probably built by Vikings; packhorse trails can also be found here. The great Pennine Way runs here too, bringing many enthusiasts to walk, run and even cycle across this wild and dangerous place.

The Anvil
BRIMHAM ROCKS

The Anvil stands dramatically silhouetted against the sky, one of a group of strangely shaped rocks on Brimham Moor.

The Domesday Book records this area as a forest, but the trees were cleared by the monks of Fountains Abbey when they first began to farm the land here. This early example of 'farming vandalism' exposed the millstone-grit outcrops and, over just a few hundred years, wind and rain, frost and ice have carved some fantastic shapes.

The rocks cover an area of about 50 acres, rising clear above the purple moor, and have attracted tourists since the 18th century. Some stand 20 feet high, and their dark and twisted forms make this look like a gallery of surreal modernistic sculptures.

Walking around these shapes it is easy to see why particular rocks have acquired their popular names, such as the 'Sphinx', 'Dancing Bear', 'Blacksmith' and the astonishing 'Idol'. The latter is a huge rock balancing on an impossibly small pedestal measuring only a foot across.

Kilnsey Crag
FROM THE PARK, WHARFEDALE

Although at 170 feet it is certainly not one of the highest features in the Dales, Kilnsey Crag is one of the best known landmarks, looming abruptly above the broad flatness of Wharfedale, and overlooking the village of Conistone across the Wharfe.

The crag leans out towards the road which runs between the river and a little beck bubbling at its foot, its ominous overhanging profile all that remains of a great spur of limestone which has been truncated and undercut by the grinding flow of glaciers. Now, it dominates the green meadows where once in ages past, a great lake glittered. The ancient green track of Mastiles Lane, which once linked Fountains Abbey with its lands to the west, runs by and the old pack horse road is still used by walkers today.

Here, Kilnsey Park Lake reflects the cottages of the small village which huddles in the shadow of the crag which, with its 40-foot overhang, is a magnet for climbing and abseiling enthusiasts, as well as film-makers.

LImesTone Pavements
RIBBLESDALE

The Limestone pavements of the Yorkshire Dales are probably its most significant feature, and can be found right across the massive limestone plateau. Some of the most extensive and best-known pavements can be seen at Malham and Souther-scales Scars.

The surface of these platforms appears to be devoid of plant life, but closer inspection will reveal the scab-like patches of lichen which are generally light grey in colour. These lichens eat into the limestone, softening the sharper edges.

Over time, soil generally builds up on bare rock, but in thousands of years this has not happened on these outcrops. Water and acid rain has dissolved the limestone, causing the grikes, and these deep and shady fissures are a haven for plants which grow untroubled by the vagaries of the weather and browsing sheep or rabbits. Harts tongue ferns and spleenworts, wood anemones and wood sorrel are all associated with damp and sheltered woodland and yet they flourish in this dry and apparently soil-less environment.

The trees that manage to grow on the pavements, are stunted by the struggle to survive, and their dark twisted forms add a surreal touch to the stark and barren rock of these lunar landscapes.

Norber Erratic
NEAR AUSTWICK

A testament to the power of the glaciers, the Norber erratics can be seen high on the limestone hillside above the village of Austwick, where they have stood, unmoving, for the 12,000 years since the end of the last Ice Age.

Erratics are rocks and boulders that were carried great distances from their original position by the moving ice sheets, and deposited in distant and very different situations. Geologists believe that these boulders at Norber probably came from Crummack Dale (about half a mile away) as there are outcrops of the same dark Silurian gritstone on the valley floor there.

There are hundreds of these ancient and sombre erratics at Norber, some of which measure up to ten feet across, contrasting strangely with the much younger white limestone. Together these create an almost primeval landscape. The 'mushrooms' were formed over long ages: the hard rock of the erratics protected the limestone beneath, while the surrounding area was weathered and eroded away; the small area of limestone under each boulder was thus preserved, forming a plinth on which these intriguing geological features seem to balance.

Malham Cove
NEAR MALHAM

Many visitors are drawn to the splendid limestone pavements which top the crag at Malham, extending for 1,000 feet. This soaring limestone cliff, that dominates the sweeping curve of Malham Cove, was formed 330 million years ago. Subsequent glaciation, alternating with warmer periods and slightly acid rainfall, dissolved the limestone, forming the clints and runnels which are the features of these pavements.

Aeons ago, a mighty waterfall plunged from the Watlowes Valley above the crag, its height exceeding that of Niagara Falls. All trace of this great cataract has disappeared and now only little Malham beck trickles along the valley floor, and meanders peacefully through the village, out of all proportion to the majesty of the crag.

Malham tarn on the moor above the cliff is an upland lake unusually formed in the porous limestone because of its impervious slate bed. Charles Kingsley came to walk here and to fish, and he found the inspiration for his 19th-century fairy tale, *The Water Babies* in the little beck.

From the tarn there is a descent through the now dry, boulder-strewn Watlowes Valley, which ends at the broad limestone plateau with its magnificent vista of upper Airedale.

Penyghent Peak
NEAR HORTON-IN-RIBBLESDALE

The steep southern 'nose' and sloping top make Penyghent easily recognisable, crouching over the flat limestone moors which surround it. Rising to 2,273 feet, this is the lowest of the trio of mountains which make up the 'Three Peaks' area of the Yorkshire Dales, and it is at Horton below Penyghent, that the famous Three Peaks Race begins and ends.

The climb to the flat, millstone grit summit is not strenuous. The Pennine Way leads over Penyghent, and those who venture here are well rewarded. The flatter parts of this hill are dotted with pot-holes, most famously 'Great Hunt Pot', while the craggy rocks are hung about with the glorious colour of purple saxifrage.

The views are quite breathtaking; a panoramic vista rolls out in all directions. Ingleborough and Whernside peaks loom up across the Ribble valley, Langstrothdale lies further to the north, and to the south-east is Fountains Fell, where the Pennine Way runs on.

Reef Knoll Limestone Boulder
RIBBLESDALE

This boulder bears a similarity to the dark gritstone erratics of Norber, however, this rock is formed from limestone, and its curious relief markings indicate that it was once part of a coral reef. When this land was covered by the shallow tropical seas that eventually formed the limestone, the warm carboniferous waters provided the ideal environment for the corals, which grew around its islands.

Many ages later these were covered by softer types of limestone and other rocks, and as the seas receded these were subject to quicker erosion. As they have been worn down, the hard reefs of coral have been exposed, especially to the south. This erosion and exposure is still going on, and these reefs will in time become more pronounced.

In Wharfedale near Thorpe, the hills of Kail, Ebolton, Stebden and Butter Haw rise up in a circle, a splendid example of reef knolls just being revealed, and providing a thought-provoking reminder of the warm lagoons and the life that teemed in them here, aeons ago.

Oxnop Scar
ABOVE ASKRIGG

The immense row of limestone crags above Oxnop Moor gleams in the sunlight, and the steep hillside drops below, littered with the scree and boulders which have been loosened by water and frost, to tumble down from the great outcrop.

Oxnop Scar stands 500 feet above sea level, and few people venture far from the high pass road which links Swaledale with Wensleydale. From the highest point of the road there are magnificent views: to the north lies Muker and the solitary building of 17th-century Low Oxnop Hall; it is certainly the most remarkable building of this period in Swaledale. To the south the moorland rolls down to Askrigg, its church rising clearly above the cottages, and Semer Water lake glitters in the far distance. Those who pause here may be rewarded by a glimpse of the golden plovers that find safe nesting sites in this undisturbed and awesome place.

Long Churn
INGLEBOROUGH

Water dives into many pot-holes of the Three Peaks district, mysteriously re-appearing in distant caves. In the days before electricity, when candles were the only source of light, these black, cavernous depths were generally given a wide berth, but there were some whose sense of adventure overcame their fear of the unknown, as long ago as the 18th century.

When the first tourists came to the Yorkshire Dales, guides would escort parties down into Long Churn on Ingleborough's slopes. They carried wooden ladders, and the blackening of the rocks in this long and winding series of caves, indicate the route these people took, carrying flaming torches. At this time the various features of these caverns were given names such as 'Dr Bannister's Handbasin' and 'St Paul's'.

This underground system was found to connect with Diccan Pot and Alum Pot which was discovered in 1847. The first people to descend into this cave used a fire escape belt and ropes and pulleys to get out. A year later, navvies who were working on the nearby Settle to Carlisle railway line erected an enormous wooden gantry over the shaft, enabling these early cavers to be lowered and raised in a large bucket.

Gordale Scar
NEAR MALHAM

Close to Malham Cove and Janet's Foss is a wide, boulder-strewn meadow and broad sky where the Gordale Scar gorge opens. At first seeming quite innocuous, dramatic limestone walls soon close in, and at the narrow head of the ravine the sheer cliffs close in ominously overhead.

It is sometimes thought that the gorge was formed when the roof of a great cave fell in, but the more probable explanation is that it was scoured out of the rocks by glacial meltwater carrying abrasive rocks and sediments.

Rocks are still occasionally hurled down here, loosened by the action of frost, and the cold and threatening atmosphere of this place has made a deep impression on its many visitors, including Turner and Wordworth. The romantic poet Thomas Gray came here in the 18th century and was reportedly quite terrified.

Rocks and boulders are piled steeply at the narrowest point of Gordale, over which a waterfall tumbles down. It varies in size, disappearing completely during dry periods, and the rocks can usually be climbed to reach the top. Now there are steps and footpaths, where the people of Malham used to graze their hardy and sure-footed little goats.

Limestone Gorge
RIVER DEE, GARSDALE

The waters of the River Dee, constantly washing over the layers of weaker shales, have created the attractive staircase effect of shallow waterfalls in the hard limestone of the river bed, and here the action of pebbles and swirling water has scooped hundreds of little hollows in the rock.

This is one of the many interesting features along the Adam Sedgewick Trail, named after the great Victorian geologist who was born in Dent, a short distance to the south. He discovered and studied the Dent Fault, which is one of the two great faults in the geological systems of the Yorkshire Dales.

Faults are enormous fractures made by ancient upheavals in the land mass, which then led to the slipping of one side so revealing the strata of rocks as they were laid down millions of years ago. The Craven Fault is actually a line of three faults which can be detected to the south of Ingleborough, at Giggleswick Scar and Malham Cove.

To the west is the Dent Fault where the more ancient Silurian slates of the Lake District meet the carboniferous limestone and Yoredale shales of the Dales; the Adam Sedgwick trail follows a fascinating route showing some of the fault's remarkable geology.

THE YORKSHIRE DALES

CUSTOMS & LEGENDS

The customs and legends of the Dales are rooted in its history and landscape. Pagan and Christian rituals are still celebrated, ghosts and trolls were said to inhabit dark caverns, and it is believed giants once occupied the soaring crags.

Hubberholme Churchyard
WHARFEDALE

Sheep graze placidly in the churchyard of St Michael, Hubberholme. Inside the little church is a plaque to the memory of J. B. Priestley, the well known author of *The Good Companions*, *An Inspector Calls* and many other works. He delighted in this church and his ashes were placed here in the graveyard.

There is a sense of timelessness all around this quiet village as the local people go about their work tending their flocks; in June and July they can be seen in the meadows, gathering hay for winter feed as generations have done before them.

Every New Year the Hubberholme Parliament sits to hold a 'candle auction'. Next to the inn, which was once the vicarage, the church owns some land known as the 'Poor Pasture', which the local farmers bid to rent for one year. The parliament consists of the 'Lords' or the lounge bar where the auctioneer (once the vicar) sits; the farmers sit in the public bar which is the 'Commons'. A candle is lit and bidding lasts until it burns out. This is a very serious auction for the land is needed, and the rent money is given to the poor.

Simon Seat
BARDEN FELL

The cluster of crags and rocks at the summit of Barden Fell provides a wonderful viewpoint above Skyreholme, which is a tributary valley of the Wharfe. There is a story that relates how a shepherd tending his flocks on Barden moor, found a baby amongst these rocks. He took the child home where, despite their poverty, the other shepherds agreed to help with the raising of the boy, each putting a little money into a fund. The child was named Simon after the man who had found him, and he acquired the surname Amang'em because the shepherds had shared his upbringing 'among them.'

Barden moor is a wild and exhilarating place to explore, but below it to the south, in contrast are the green and pleasant environs of Bolton Priory and the sheltered climate of Strid woods. Immediately beneath the high fell is Posforth Gill, in medieval times this area was an old deer park. Now it is called 'The Valley of Desolation' because it was once laid waste by a great landslip. Time passed and although the valley recovered to become a very pleasant place, it still retains its ominous-sounding name.

The Burning of Owd Bartle
WEST WITTON

It is said that a wicked giant once inhabited the heights of Pen Hill above West Witton, but he met his end when the ghost of a young girl that he had slaughtered caused his own great dog to attack him, sending him over the precipice.

These days the people of West Witton enjoy their annual festivities untroubled by any evil presence. On the nearest Saturday to the 24th August the villagers celebrate with a 'feast' or festival, when gardens are opened to the public and there is a 'fell race' up Pen Hill. In the evening, a huge bonfire is lit for 'The Burning of Owd Bartle', when an effigy is burned. The 24th August is St Bartholomew's feast day, although the custom probably has its origins in pre-Christian times.

The cottages of West Witton were once dotted solely along the high roadside, but the rising population during the 18th and 19th centuries, has resulted in a continuous linear village that stretches for almost a mile. The old road to West Burton and a field path provide a pleasant walk up to the 1,844-feet-high summit of Pen Hill, and one of the most breathtaking aerial views in the Dales.

Leyburn Shawl
LEYBURN

The path behind the grand ancient house of Thornborough Hall in Leyburn leads out onto a ridge of grass and trees known as 'The Leyburn Shawl'. This provides a splendid platform, looking out on a spectacular view of Wensleydale, with seats to allow visitors the luxury of lingering in comfort. The walk was laid out in the last century, and became a fashionable promenade. The famed 'Leyburn Tea Festival' took place here, and attracted great crowds; in 1845 more than 3,000 people came to enjoy the tea and dancing.

There are several paths to follow from the Shawl, all of which afford very pleasant walks. One of these runs through the Bolton Park Estate and on to Bolton Castle and its village. 'Queen's Gap' is said to be the place where Mary, Queen of Scots was recaptured after escaping from Bolton Castle where she had been imprisoned. Stories of her escape also allege that, as she fled, she dropped her shawl, thus giving the place its name.

Hornblower
BAINBRIDGE

The Bainbridge horn-blower wears his uniform to blow his horn at nine o'clock every evening. It is said that the sound of the horn guided travellers to the safety of the village after dark, in the days when packs of wolves ran in the forests hereabouts. The custom probably has less philanthropic origins, however. After the Conquest, the Normans began to seize land all over Yorkshire including great tracts of what is now the Yorkshire Dales. The people took great exception to this appropriation, and resisted strongly. The rebellion was ferociously put down during the 'Harrying of the North' which reached parts of the Dales, and the people suffered terrible persecution. In establishing their authority, the Norman rulers introduced measures to control the population, including curfews to curtail poaching in their hunting preserves.

Some of these rules have been passed on as customs which continue to be preserved today. An example of this is the blowing of three blasts on the Bainbridge curfew horn, which has been carried out by several generations of the Metcalfe family.

Bridge over the Bain
SEMERWATER

This triple-arched bridge spans the river Bain, the shortest river in the Dales. It is the outflow for the largest natural lake in the Dales: Semer Water, whose calm beauty has provided a spiritual and artistic inspiration for many.

In 1956, the vicar of Askrigg held the first open air service here from a 'floating pulpit'; this continues today. On the Sunday of every August Bank Holiday weekend, the vicar stands in a boat and preaches to a congregation gathered on the shores.

Turner came here frequently, and his watercolour of Semerwater (or Simmer Lake as he knew it) is now in the British Museum. In the centre of the foreground of the picture is a huge boulder, this is the Carlin stone which rests on the lake's shores, and is reputed to have been thrown by the devil – though geologists claim it was deposited by a glacier.

A beautiful city is said to have stood here, but was drowned after a curse. It is claimed that sometimes, when the lake is still and silent, the ringing of bells can be heard coming from the city beneath the water.

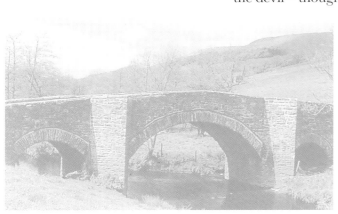

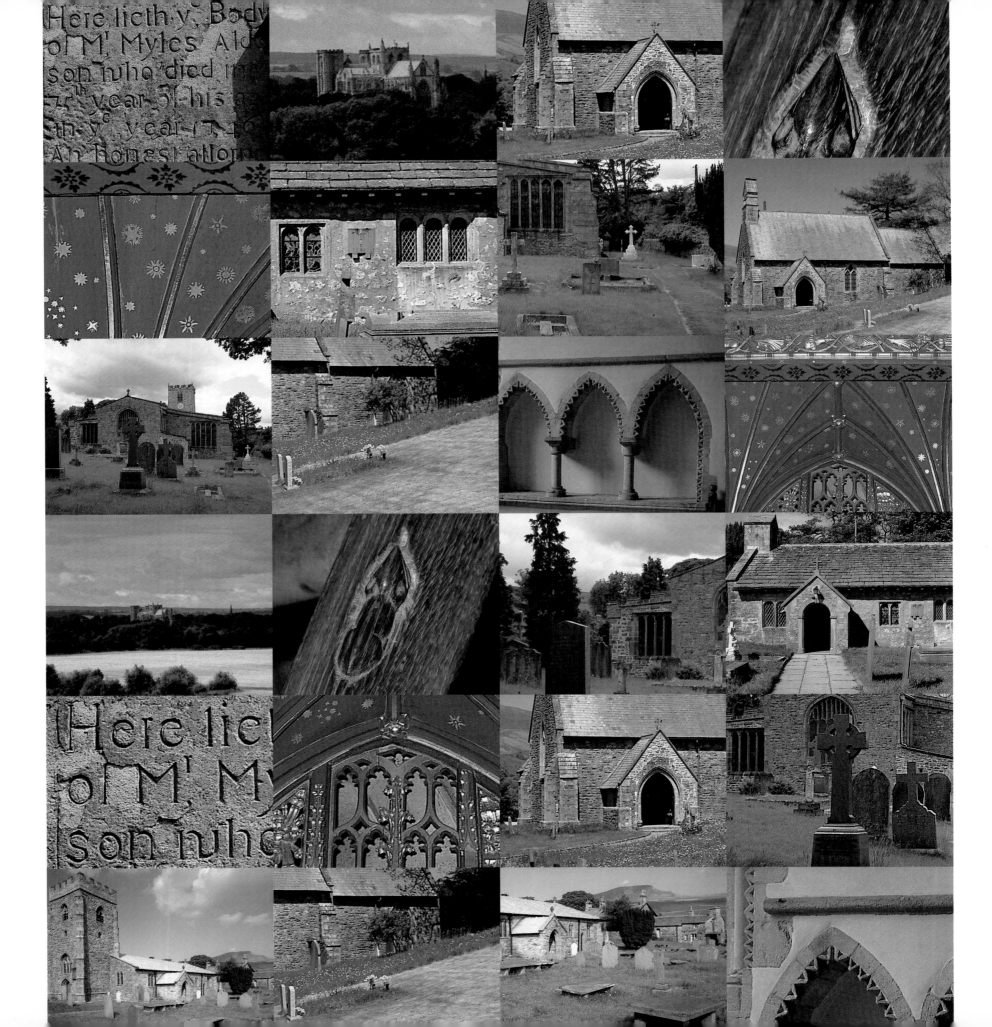

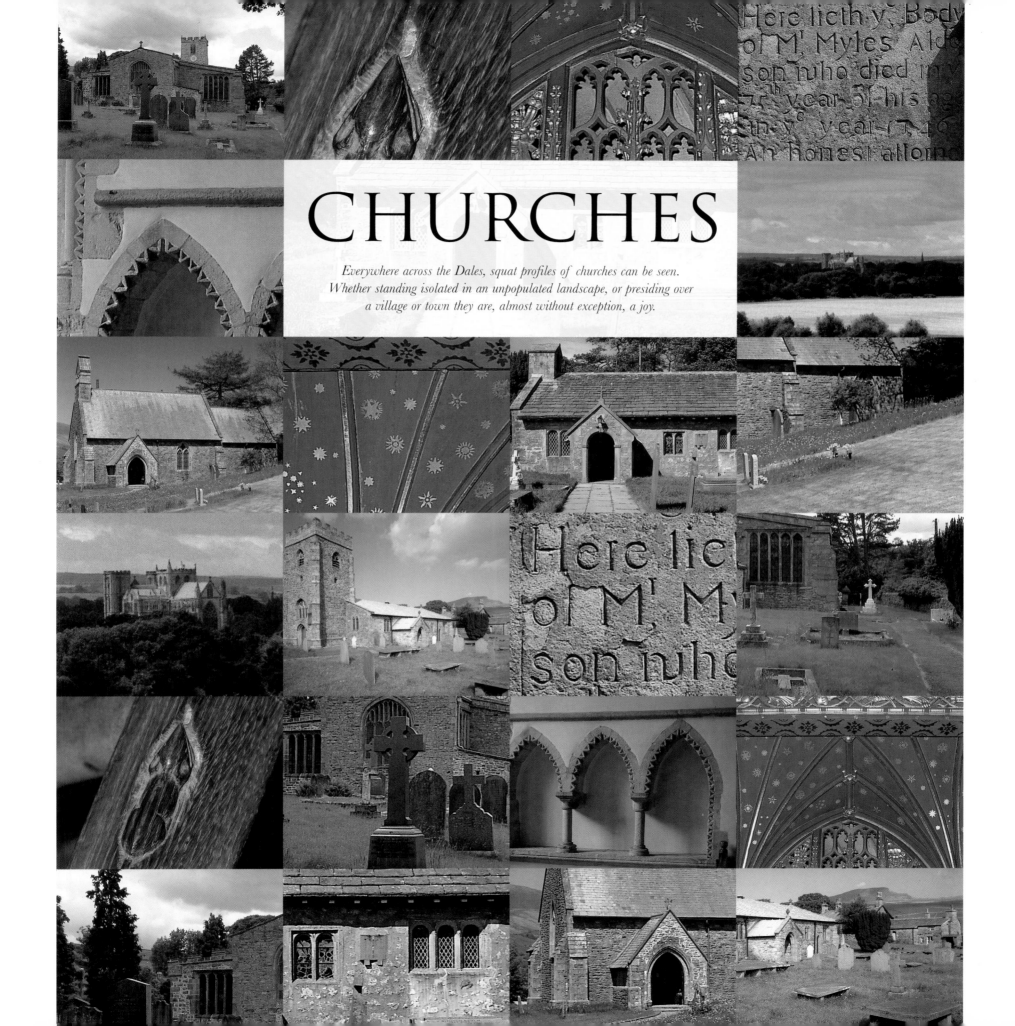

CHURCHES

*Everywhere across the Dales, squat profiles of churches can be seen.
Whether standing isolated in an unpopulated landscape, or presiding over
a village or town they are, almost without exception, a joy.*

St Andrew's Church
GRINTON

The extensive parish of Grinton once covered the whole of Swaledale, and for the people who travelled miles to the Sunday services, a regular fair was held afterwards. There is an ancient track from Keld at the head of the dale which leads to Grinton, it is known as the 'Corpse Way'. Its name derives from the era when the deceased of remote villages and farms were carried along this path in wicker baskets to be buried in the churchyard.

St Andrew's church is probably situated on an ancient pagan site and was built by monks of Bridlington. There has been a church here for 900 years and some original features remain, although the building dates mostly from the 13th to the 15th centuries. It has all the peace and atmosphere of centuries of worship. There are some superb stained glass windows which are a mixture of Medieval and Victorian, and an intriguing narrow window is set in the wall, giving a view from outside of a side altar. This is known as the 'leper's squint' because, through this small slit, those afflicted with the disease could observe the service without entering the church and spreading the contagion.

St Leonard's Chapel
CHAPEL-LE-DALE

The exquisite little chapel of St Leonard is barely 50 feet long; it was built in the 17th century on the site on an ancient chapel of ease for Ingleton, which gave the village its name. Chapels of ease were small, subordinate churches in areas whose mother church would cover a vast and

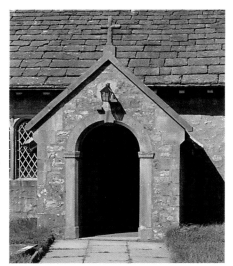

dispersed parish, as was common in the Dales at one time. There is some superb stained glass here, but most memorable is the touchingly worded plaque in honour of the hundreds of men who died building the Settle to Carlisle railway.

Christopher Long, the man who discovered the nearby White Scar Cave in 1923 is buried here. This show cave is the most impressive in the Dales, with a magnificent display of stalactites and stalagmites, some of which date back 225,000 years.

Chapel-le-Dale is tucked into the foot of Ingleborough, and nearby are many echoing caves and nightmarish pot-holes which have inevitably given rise to ghost stories. Above the church, Hurtle Pot is said to be haunted by a loathsome Boggart who drowns his victims in its waters.

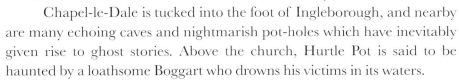

St Michael's Church
HUBBERHOLME

The little village of Hubberholme is hidden away from the main highway beside the River Wharfe, but its church is renowned. There is a unique charm about St Michael and All the Angels for there is a remarkable blending of ancient and modern in its simple interior. The new window in the south wall shows, in glowing colours, the history of the parish, and the simple 20th-century oak pews were made by Robert Thompson, 'The Mouse Man of Kilburn'. It is entertaining to search for his carved 'signature' mice, which can be found running up and down the pews.

Above Robert Thompson's handiwork hangs one of the greatest treasures of the Yorkshire Dales, a splendid rood-loft. Painted red, black and gold and dating from 1558 it is one of only two to survive after an edict of 1571, which decreed that all rood-lofts should be destroyed. Hubberholme's loft escaped destruction simply because of its position in this quiet little backwater.

Originally a forest chapel, this unassuming little church is imbued with a timeless peace which made it J. B. Priestley's favourite place, and probably one of the greatest delights in the Dales.

St Oswald's Church
ASKRIGG

This weather-worn old gravestone was placed in Askrigg churchyard in 1713 and is apparently the oldest legible memorial to be found here. It has been hung on the church wall now, where it is protected from further erosion by the slates which have been set above it.

Askrigg has been settled continuously since prehistoric times, but until the building of a church here in the 12th century, the Christian population had to worship and be buried at Aysgarth. St Oswald's is a typically low-profile Dales church and is a very fine example of the perpendicular style, with a splendid vaulted tower and remarkable beamed ceiling in the nave. The north aisle was added in the 15th century, and the south aisle was restored in 1770. The zealous Victorian parishioners replaced the furnishings and added other embellishments.

In this graveyard lie those like the 'Honest Attorney' who had the worldly means to ensure the kind of immortality afforded by the old stones. Alongside them rest those countless hard-working Dalesfolk whose only memorial must be the landscape that they helped to shape.

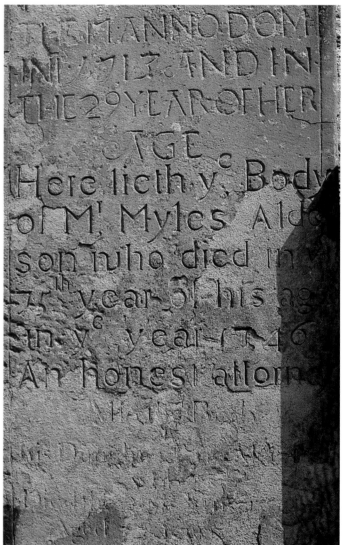

St Mark's Church
CAUTLEY

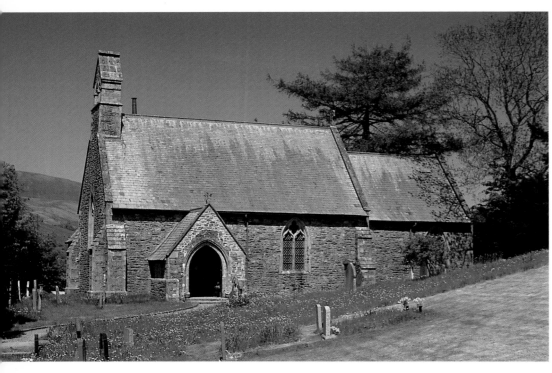

St Mark's at Cautley is a tiny church built to serve a very sparse population and is hidden away from the road, close to Cautley Spout. The immense Howgill Fells rise as a backdrop, dotted with dark trees and white sheep, making this one of the most delightfully positioned churches in the Dales.

After the arrival of the Normans, and with the establishment of the monasteries, many churches were built in the Dales. Some of these Norman churches were built on existing sites where earlier churches had stood, but before this time, one Mother Church would generally have served a huge parish. For example, Aysgarth church had a parish of 80,000 acres, and the evidence of the long distances that the faithful had to tread, can be seen in the miles of narrow footpaths which thread across the land to converge at that church.

During the Dark Ages, courageous missionaries had come to even the most remote parts of this land. They braved the wild animals who roamed the great forests here, to preach the Christian message at particular places marked by preaching crosses, and this isolated little church may well be situated where one of these once stood.

St Andrew's Church
AYSGARTH

This beautiful screen is one of two which can be seen in St Andrew's Church at Aysgarth. Originally these outstanding examples of medieval woodwork were made for Jervaulx Abbey, probably at Ripon, and were brought here after the Dissolution during which the Abbey was almost razed to the ground.

Overlooking the Upper Falls, Aysgarth Church is a typical Victorian edifice. Built in 1866 on older foundations, its four-acre churchyard is the largest in England and its great size seems incongruous in this setting. There

are only a few houses, an inn and an old mill nearby, but for centuries this was the Mother Church for a large part of Wensleydale, and a great number of footpaths converge here.

Aysgarth village is reached by a path which passes over fields above the bend in the river with a birds-eye view of the falls. The pretty village has a tiny green, on which stood the village stocks, and owes its unspoilt charm to its distance from the tourist attraction of the waterfalls.

St Oswald's Church
HORTON-IN-RIBBLESDALE

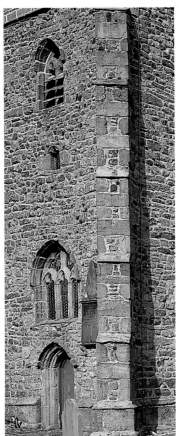

The massive scar of Beecroft Quarry looms over the village of Horton-in-Ribblesdale. Situated between Ingleborough and Penyghent, it has become a popular centre for the walkers who come along the Pennine Way, and for adventurers lured by the danger and exhilaration of the surrounding limestone countryside. This is where the various races which take place over the Three Peaks begin and end. Horton also has a very intriguing church. St Oswald's dates from Norman times as can be seen from its doorway, and was once the Mother Church for Ribblesdale. Its roof is made from Dales lead and there are some splendid examples of stained glass. Of particular note is a small and ancient depiction of Thomas à Becket.

One of the most notable features of this church is the way it leans. A glance at the angle of the pillars can seem worrying, but they have been leaning like this for generations and the building is in no danger of suddenly collapsing. A definite slant can be discerned in many east windows of the churches in the Dales, but none display an entire interior that leans as St Oswald's does.

Holy Trinity Church
WENSLEY

This fine old triple Sedilia, for the use of clergy, is set close to the altar of Holy Trinity Church in Wensley. This lovely old church was built in 1245 on the site of a Saxon church, and stones from that ancient building, dating from 760, are set in one wall. There have been some additions to Holy Trinity over the centuries, including a modern side altar, but since the raising of the chancel and aisle walls in the 15th century, the church stands much as it did 700 years ago. The only Victorian addition is the sundial.

The interior has many interesting features: 13th-century windows and heraldic shields, early 14th-century murals, a lovely ornamental 15th-century screen, and 18th-century stalls.

John Wesley preached here, and Frances l'Anson, the original 'Sweet lass of Richmond Hill', was baptised in the 17th-century font. The church's connection with Bolton Hall, whose gates are close by, began with the powerful Scrope family of Bolton Castle, long before the Dissolution; their family pew can still be seen in the church.

This is one of the most outstanding churches in the Dales, and its pale stone gleams warmly from an airy position above Wensleydale, beside the pretty cottages of Wensley village.